# HYPSILOPHODON

by Janet Riehecky
illustrated by Ching

THE CHILD'S WORLD

MANKATO, MN

*Grateful appreciation is expressed to
Bret S. Beall, Research Consultant,
Field Museum of Natural History, Chicago,
Illinois, who reviewed this book to
insure its accuracy.*

**Library of Congress Cataloging in Publication Data**

Riehecky, Janet, 1953-
   Hypsilophodon / by Janet Riehecky ; illustrated by Ching.
      p. cm. — (Dinosaur books)
   Summary: Describes the physical characteristics, habits, and
natural environment of the small dinosaur whose build suggests that
it was a swift runner.
   ISBN 0-89565-628-0 (lib. bdg.)
   1. Hypsilophodon—Juvenile literature.   [1. Hypsilophodon.
2. Dinosaurs.]   I. Ching, ill.   II. Title.   III. Series: Riehecky,
Janet, 1953-          Dinosaur books.
QE862.O65R528    1990
567.9'7—dc20                                              90-2520
                                                              CIP
                                                               AC

# HYPSILOPHODON

Did you ever wonder what a dinosaur's day was like? Well, most dinosaurs probably spent their days trying to find enough food to eat.

But do you suppose that sometimes dinosaurs took time out from eating just to have fun?

Maybe little dinosaurs tumbled and wrestled, playing together.

Duckbilled dinosaurs may have rolled in the mud, just because it felt so good.

Big dinosaurs may have plunged into a lake for a cool, relaxing swim.

And meat eaters may have enjoyed an
afternoon nap after a big lunch.

No one can say for sure whether or not dinosaurs had fun. But if they did, the Hypsilophodon (HIP-sih-LOW-fo-don) probably had fun running.

The Hypsilophodon was a small, graceful dinosaur. Scientists think its long legs and narrow feet made it a swift runner. Imagine it streaking across an open field or plunging through the undergrowth in a forest—running for the sheer joy of it.

Of course, even if the Hypsilophodon did run just for fun, it probably spent more time running for its life! The Hypsilophodon lived in a dangerous world, full of fierce meat eaters. Against such enemies, the Hypsilophodon would have had a tough time defending itself. It grew only six or seven feet tall, and weighed only about one hundred and thirty pounds. That's smaller than many people. Hypsilophodon did have sharp claws on its feet, but they weren't very big compared to the huge claws of many meat eaters. If a Hypsilophodon saw a meat eater coming, it needed to RUN!

*long, stiff tail*

The Hypsilophodon had strong leg muscles and a slender body. Scientists think it could run as fast as thirty miles per hour. Its tail had special bones which kept it quite stiff. This helped the Hypsilophodon to keep its balance while running. It also might have been helpful when the Hypsilophodon was trying to dodge a meat eater. Some scientists think the dinosaur could change directions quickly by swinging its tail to one side.

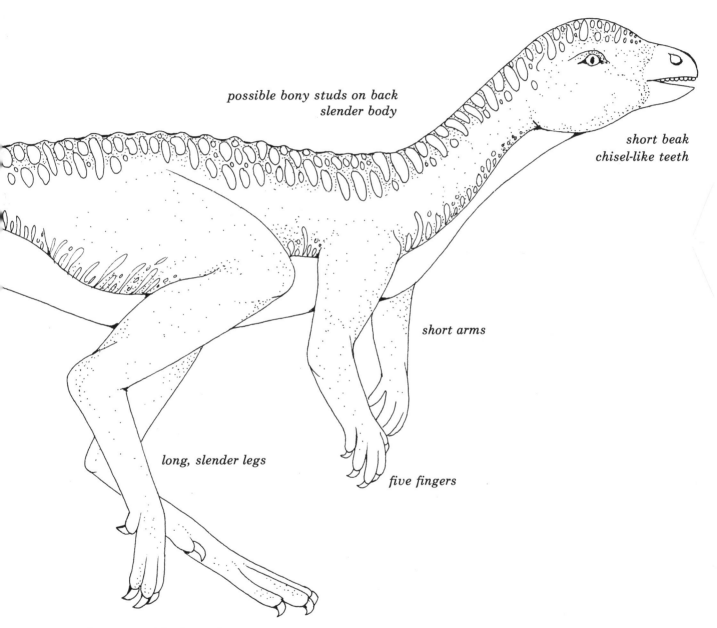

possible bony studs on back
slender body

short beak
chisel-like teeth

short arms

long, slender legs

five fingers

four toes with sharp claws

Another of Hypsilophodon's favorite activities, besides running, was eating. It was a plant eater, and its mouth was just right for chomping all kinds of plants. It had a sharp beak with a few teeth in front and more teeth in the cheek. The name Hypsilophodon means "high-ridged tooth." It was named that because its teeth were sharply ridged, like chisels. They could handle the toughest meal.

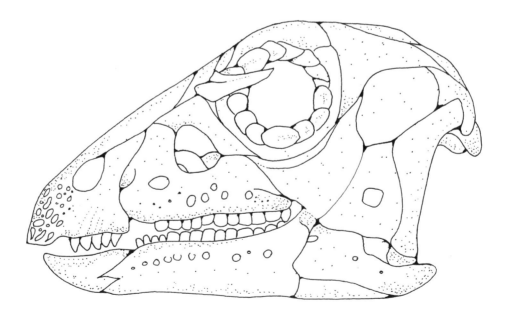

Like many other plant eaters, Hypsilophodons probably lived and traveled in herds. Scientists once found over twenty Hypsilophodon skeletons all together in one spot. Perhaps part of a herd got caught in a flash flood or trapped in some quicksand.

All the skeletons were of adult Hypsilophodons. Scientists aren't sure why there weren't any babies. It could be that the adults and babies did not stay together. Or maybe the babies were able to avoid whatever disaster trapped their parents.

Scientists aren't sure how Hypsilophodons treated their babies, but some think Hypsilophodons returned to the same place every time they were ready to lay their eggs. The mother Hypsilophodons probably laid eggs in spiral circles on the ground. Each group of eggs was probably about eight feet from the next. Adults may have watched over the eggs until they hatched. Scientists believe the babies did not stay in the nests after they hatched. They think the babies were born ready to go and left to look for food on the very day they were born.

Where did the scientists get these ideas? They found a nesting ground of a dinosaur that is closely related to the Hypsilophodon. The groups of eggs in that nesting ground were laid in spiral circles. The distances between groups of eggs was about equal to the length of an adult. Scientists think the adults laid their eggs that far apart so that they could walk through the "aisles," guarding the eggs.

In the groups of eggs that the scientists found, only the top part of each eggshell was broken. Scientists think this means the babies broke out of their shells and left right away. If the babies had stayed in the nest, the shells would have been broken to bits, crushed by the babies walking over and over them. Skeletons of the babies which were almost ready to hatch show that they were strong enough to walk right after they were born.

Scientists try to be careful about sounding too sure when they describe how the Hypsilophodon lived. That's because they've been wrong in the past.

When the first Hypsilophodon skeleton was found, an artist sketched the bones so that scientists could study them. For some reason, he twisted the first claw on each foot so that it faced backwards. The toes of the Hypsilophodon then looked like the toes of many birds.

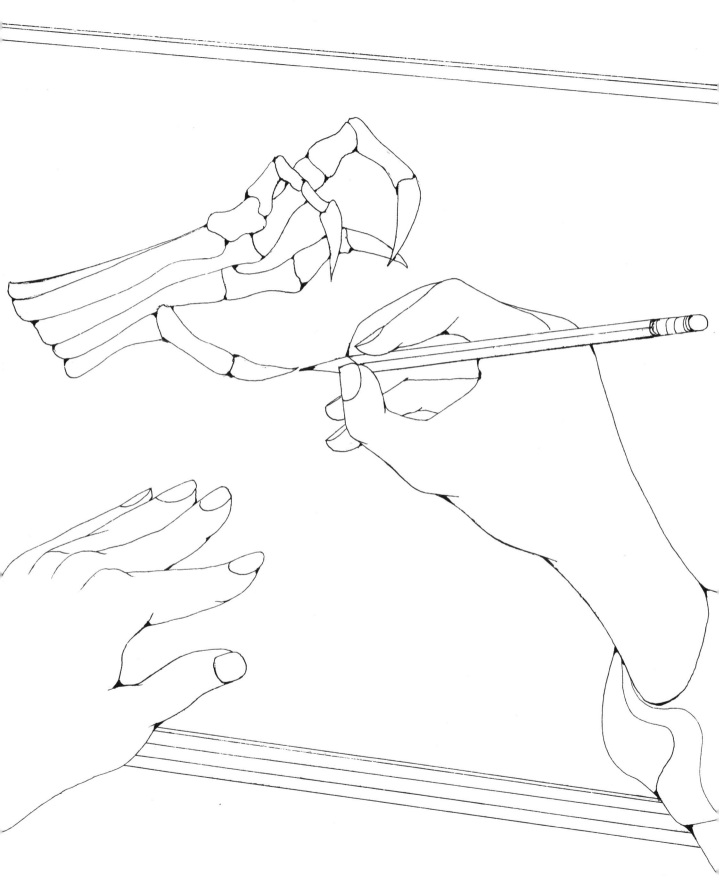

Scientists who studied the sketch sug-
gested that, like birds, Hypsilophodons
might have used their backward-facing
toes to hold onto branches. The scientists
pictured Hypsilophodons spending much

of their lives in the trees. They described
how they thought this small dinosaur
jumped from branch to branch, using its
tail for balance.

Then the scientists discovered the mistake the artist had made. Suddenly the idea of a tree-hopping dinosaur sounded pretty silly. As the scientists studied the legs and feet of the Hypsilophodon more carefully, they noticed that their legs were built exactly like the legs of the animals alive today that are very fast runners. So, the scientists changed their ideas about the Hypsilophodon.

Some new discovery may make the scientists change their minds again. But in the meantime, you can have fun using the information we have to imagine how the Hypsilophodon spent its days.

## Dinosaur Fun

One way that scientists can tell if a dinosaur was a fast runner is by studying its footprints. To show how important that evidence can be, you will need the help of your pet dog!

First, get your pet to walk through water or mud. (Your mother would probably prefer you use water.) Then direct your pet to first walk, then run on a sidewalk.

How are the "walking" footprints different from the "running" footprints? What do you think scientists would say about a small dinosaur whose footprints were far apart?